Voodoo

An Introductory Guide

History, Beliefs, Elements, Strains or Schools, Practices, Myths and Facts

By Riley Star

Copyrights and Trademarks

Disclaimer and Legal Notice

Foreword

Voodoo is probably one of the most misunderstood religions in the world - owing to sensationalist misrepresentations in popular culture and the entertainment media. But perhaps our misunderstanding of this religion also stems from the relatively little public knowledge there is in what Voodoo really is. We have a sense that Voodoo is what we see in the movies, and we have no immediate need to determine what is actually fact or fantasy, thus tacitly accepting what we think we know.

But this is a grave disservice - especially to the West African slaves who were brought to the Americas during the course of the Atlantic Slave trade, and for whom Voodoo has been a revitalizing and energizing spiritual influence. Voodoo reminded them of their roots, their true identities beyond slavery, and it gave them the strength of purpose to fight for - and win - their freedom.

Hopefully, the age of ignorance and prejudice will soon recede with the open mind with which many people now view many of the older religions, Voodoo included. It is to be hoped that this book would also assist in our edification of the public perception and knowledge regarding this ancient African religion.

Table of Contents

Introduction...1

Chapter One: What is Voodoo..................................5

What is Voodoo 5

History of Voodoo...6

Chapter Two: Elements of Voodoo.........................11

Belief in a Divine Creator 12

Vodoo Spirits, Animism, and Ancestor Worship 13

Belief in a Soul...16

Rituals, Priests and Priestesses.............................16

Talismans and Fetishes..17

Chapter Three: The Different Strains of Voodoo 19

West African Voodoo...20

Demographics of Voodoo Faithful in West Africa 20

The Spiritual Life of West Africa.......................21

Chapter Four: Vodou in the Caribbean..........................23

Caribbean Vodou...23

Haitian Revolution and the Bois Caiman Ceremony 26

The Bois Caiman Ceremony of August 1791.................27

Demographics of the Voodoo Faithful in the Caribbean..28

The Spiritual Life of Vodou in the Caribbean 29

Chapter Five: Louisiana Voodoo................................33

Louisiana Voodoo 34

Demographics of Voodoo Faithful in Louisiana............... 37

The Spiritual Life of Louisiana Voodoo 38

Chapter Six: The Dark Side of Voodoo 41

Curses, Poisons and Hexes 43

Voodoo Dolls.. 44

Zombies.. 45

Juju and Hoodoo.. 49

Chapter Seven: Voodoo and Racism 53

Catholic and Christian Prejudices.......................... 54

Ignorance, Fear, and Racism 55

Chapter Eight: Voodoo Myths and Facts 59

Voodoo Myths... 59

Voodoo Facts.. 61

Index.. 65

Photo Credits... 69

References.. 71

Introduction

Voodoo, also known as Vodou or Vodoun, is an indigenous religion of the West African peoples. The term "voodoo" itself translates to "spirit" or "Great Spirit," and as we will learn during the course of this book, the power and veneration of spirits - whether of nature spirits who are included in the African pantheons, or of the spirits of the ancestors of a clan or tribe - are central to most Voodoo religious practice and belief.

The Voodoo faithful also believe in a Supreme Being, but one who is also aloof and distant from human affairs. Thus this Supreme Being granted powers to several spirits (some stories say that they are sons of the Mawi, the Divine Creator), and they are each tasked with the different aspects of life and nature. They also serve as the mediators between the world of the living and the world of the spirits, so most contact that humans have with the divine is through the spirits or "Loas," whose powers, wisdom, and guidance they seek and invoke through offerings, dances, prayers, songs and rituals. The dead ancestors of the different tribes or clans are also honored spirits, and it is to them that the living turn for wisdom and guidance, as well as for protection and healing.

With a generational wisdom that honors and reveres the spirits of both the dead and the spirits of nature - why is it most of what the public knows of Voodoo is negative? Zombies, voodoo dolls with pins sticking out of them, curses, spells, hexes, jinxes, and ceremonial dances and music done in the shadows of the night, dark magic, dark sorcery, and worship of strange and devilish gods. The very term voodoo itself, taken with all the connotations that have been ingrained in our minds with films and other sensationalist literature - the word voodoo is enough to strike terror into the hearts of many people who do not know better.

If it is simply a matter of not knowing enough because there was simply no good information available to the public, then books such as this, with the many articles, documentaries, and journalist reports that have since been available to the public in recent years should be a good start to dispelling many of the misconceptions and false assumptions about Voodoo. Voodoo is now widely recognized as a legitimate religion, with its own cosmology, worldview, and spiritual beliefs, practices and traditions of the West African people.

As you continue reading through the pages of this book, we will learn about the spread, evolution of growth of Voodoo, which is essentially inseparable from the Atlantic slave trade which led to the oppression and abuse of millions of West Africans who were brought to the Americas in the most dismal and miserable conditions. And with the lives of slavery and lowly servitude awaiting them in the lands where they were brought to, one of the things that the West African slaves clung to was their indigenous religious beliefs - and Voodoo was certainly one of the more prominent.

Voodoo experienced a rebirth in conditions of slavery, so perhaps the darkness associated with this religion is not very difficult to understand. Slavery was a dark time for the West African slaves, and for human history as a whole. This was a time when prejudice, fear, bigotry, and racism were prevalent, driving some of the worst human rights violations that ever befell a people - save perhaps for the Holocaust. And so stories of savage rites, devilish pacts, and magical curses and hexes were easily fed to western and European minds who were ready to assume the worst of others.

Stories grew upon stories, each one feeding the others as easily as it also fed on people's fears and sense of horror.

And yet all the time, Voodoo was there, reminding the slaves and their descendants of who they once were, the free lands of their birth, the music and the songs that flowed through their bodies, the beauty that could exist in a harmonious environment, and the courage and individual worth they could derive from the blessings and protection of their revered spirits.

To this day, the Western world still does not know as much as it could of this religion. Because Voodoo is essentially an oral tradition, there are no writings we can turn to if we wish to know more about what Voodoo is. The most that we can do is listen to those who actually practice Voodoo and what they can tell us of this spiritual system. Of course, the accounts and explanations will likely be different depending on the region and the people you are speaking to - the practice of Voodoo in West Africa is not precisely the same as it is in Haiti or Louisiana.

But inroads to the mysteries of this indigenous African belief system are beginning. In this book, we have brought together some of the more widely accepted core beliefs and elements of Voodoo practice, presenting them as much as possible from the perspective of those who practice them. May this be for you an enlightening and interesting read.

Chapter One: What is Voodoo

What is Voodoo

"Voodoo" is an indigenous West African religious and spiritual system that has been spread and disseminated throughout the rest of the world with the forced migration of Western African peoples through the Atlantic Slave trade that operated from the 15th to the 17th centuries.

Voodoo is an African term for "spirit," and this belief system essentially combines animism, nature worship, and ancestory worship, together with a belief in a Supreme Being and in spirits (also called Loas or Iwas) that actively intervene in the world of the living. Much of Voodoo practices and traditions are centered around the honor and reverence given these spirits, who are thus invoked for the guidance, wisdom and protection which they bestow upon the living.

While the basic philosophies of Voodoo seems simple enough, the evolution of the practice and growth of Voodoo throughout the years can be traced by following the fate of those West Africans captured and sold as slaves, and who were thereafter brought to America. This chapter contains a brief historical background of Voodoo, and is followed by more specific regional and historical developments in later chapters.

History of Voodoo

Not much is really known about the origins of Voodoo other than that it originated in Africa, and that its pattern of dissemination throughout the rest of the world, as well as its consequent evolution, is closely tied with the history of the Atlantic slave trade.

Some claim that Voodoo is an ancient spiritual practice, and is as old as humanity itself. A tall claim - but not so implausible when you consider that Africa is considered to be the oldest inhabited territory on earth, and according to most paleontologists, is also the continent from which the human species originated.

But Africa at present is a diverse continent consisting of 54 states, thousands of languages spoken, a great number of indigenous groups, and a wide variety of religious beliefs. Africa has a very long history of contact with other countries, many of which brought their cultures and religions with them. Some say that Voodoo originated in the Slave Coast of West Africa, specifically the country Benin (formerly Dahomey), but this is likely due to the fact that the Atlantic slave trade grew from developments in seafaring technologies that allowed European seafarers to navigate the Atlantic Ocean, thus bringing them into contact with societies and settlements along the West African coast, from what is now Senegal and Gambia to the Congo region. This promoted a new route for the slave trade from the African continent to the New World of North and South America.

At this time, the major religions of Christianity and Islam already existed in Africa - brought by the expanding civilizations of the early Roman empire and early Arabian Islamic Caliphates. These two major religions coexisted with the traditional African religions - including Voodoo. These days, the diversity of religious beliefs in Africa is still the same, although it is now mixed in with small smatterings of Africans who are Hindu, Jews, Buddhists, Confucians, and Baha'i. Many of the basic practices of Voodoo are traditional - utilizing a mixture of earth and spirit worship, animism, mysticism, ancestor worship, deities, as well as ritualistic practices.

It is estimated that some 10.24 million African slaves were brought to the Americas during the height of the Atlantic slave trade, some 3 million of which were exported out of the coast of Benin - and this lasted from 1650 to 1900, until the eventual abolition of slavery and the worldwide outlawing of slavery. This was later followed by voluntary migration of Africans as freed men, crossing the Atlantic in great numbers in what is now known as a new wave or cycle of the African diaspora. Whether slave or freedmen however, the Africans brought with them their culture and way of life, including their traditional religious practices, including Voodoo.

In fact, long centuries of enforced slavery and servitude to European masters in the Americas and the West Indies had created what might be considered optimal conditions for the embracing of Voodoo - and Voodoo has undergone its own rebirth as it is practiced today in different parts of the world. While in its original essence it is still being practiced today in its home ground of West Africa, Voodoo has evolved in the lands of the New World where it took new root among the displaced Africans. Part of it may have been due to the conditions of slavery itself, and the necessary secrecy of practicing a slave religion that was suppressed by many of the European masters. But part of

Voodoo's evolution was also a result of syncretism - with Christianity and indigenous American traditions - and is a living religion practiced today in countries such as Haiti, Puerto Rico, Cuba, the Dominican Republic, Brazil, and Louisiana. Though it is certaily interesting to note that the growth, practice and development of Voodoo in each of these areas is quite different.

Chapter Two: Elements of Voodoo

Throughout the years, Voodoo has proven itself to be an adaptable, growing, and evolving religion - a testament, perhaps, to the resilience of the Africans who were sold in slavery and who kept its practice alive throughout their servitude. But Voodoo is perhaps also one of the most misunderstood religions in the world - mainly because what little we know of it is based on what we have seen in films or read about in books. But all of it is fiction and their sole purpose is to entertain.

But while none of these fictional accounts presume to teach factual history, the impression it has made on the public mind certainly has been remarkable. Perhaps because

Voodoo rituals are so rich in color, so different in context, language, and worldview from the main world religions, that people cannot help but be impressed by these selected presentations of what are really only small portions of this religion. These days, the word Voodoo raises images of zombies and dolls with pins sticking out of them - but this is only what media has conditioned our minds to automatically assume when we hear the word voodoo.

In this chapter, we take a closer look at some of the essential elements of the practice of Voodoo, its cosmology, and how it affects and influences the lifestyle and worldview of its practitioners.

Belief in a Divine Creator

Even before the arrival of the major religions of Christianity and Islam, the Voudons believed in a supreme being or a divine creator which they call Mahou, or Mawu. This is a transcendent Supreme Being, the creator of the universe and the world.

But this divine being does not figure prominently in people's lives. Probably because of his very transcendence, a person can only form a relationship with this divine being, in fact, through the intercession of spirits. Many of the practices of Voodoo faithful are thus centered around their relationship with spirits or the Vodun.

The god Mawu is omnipotent, but essentially aloof from the concerns of man. He is both unknowable and remote from worldly affairs. But Mawu delegated his powers to the Voduns or the spirits. In essence, the Voduns are Mawu's representatives on earth, and all acts of the Voduns are essentially attributable to Mawu. But his very transcendence keeps him inexplicable and incomprehensible to people, and so one cannot really find any direct worship of this divine being in Voodoo practices, save from scattered and vague references such as "God will act," or "God decides."

Vodoo Spirits, Animism, and Ancestor Worship

Voodoo practitioners believe in a Divine Creator, but this god is a distant figure that one can only communicate with through the spirits. So spirits and spirit communication is more prominent in Voodoo practice over an all-powerful deity. The term voodoo, in fact, literally means "spirit" in the local Fon language of modern day Benin.

Voodoo practitioners believe in the power of spirits, which have influence over nature and human existence. Each of the many spirits are responsible for the various domains or facets of life. There are thousands of spirits, which are called "Loa" or "Iwa," some of which are the souls of the deceased. These spirits can also act as intermediaries between the living and God. This central belief in the power of spirits seems to be a unique combination of animism and ancestor worship, where the spirits of dead ancestors and the spirits of natural elements are powerful forces to which a person can turn to for help.

Many of the actual practices of the Voodoo faithful are actually centered around their relationship with spirits. And contact with spirits is direct - the most direct of which, perhaps, is spirit possession. When a person becomes possessed by a spirit, he becomes the god himself. The spirits incarnate in the body of the person possessed, thus enabling the spirit to literally walk among the living.

This is perhaps what gave rise to the concept of zombies - or of the dead walking among the living. This is believed to take place during ritualistic dances which venerate the spirit of their ancestors - and the power of the dead who are once again brought to life are so great that it is believed that touching one who is possessed of a spirit will be enough to kill you.

There are Voduns who were once living - the spirits of dead ancestors who are often considered clan protectors. Ancestors who have passed on are believed to exist as spirits capable of interceding in human affairs. This particular element of Voodoo has always been present, but it is possible that it grew more prominent when the African slaves found themselves in conditions of forced servitude in a new land, strange surroundings, and were then expected to adopt a foreign religion. As they sought the familiar of their own traditional beliefs, they also turned to the spirits of their ancestors for help in surviving what must have been a very painful transition.

Other spirits are considered the "sons of Mawu," of which there are a great number. But we can identify at least seven of those which are considered most important:

- **Sakpata** - the eldest son, and the Vodun of the earth, of illness and healing, and to whom the earth was entrusted, represented by black, white and red spots, as well as scissors
- **Xêvioso (*or* Xêbioso)** - the Vodun of the sky, and also of justice, and is represented by a thunderbolt, the ram, fire, and the double axe
- **Agbe** - the Vodun of the sea, and is represented by a serpent, considered a symbol of life
- **Gu** - the Vodun of iron and war, and metes out justice even to accomplices of those guilty of acts of infamy
- **Agê** - the Vodun of agriculture, forests, animals and birds
- **Jo** - the Vodun of air and invisibility
- **Lêgba** - the youngest son, and a Vodun who received no gifts because these had already been spread out among his elder brothers. He is

therefore jealous, a wild card among the pantheon, thus he is considered Vodun of the unpredictable, of all else that cannot be assigned to the others, of daily tragedies and unforeseen events

These sons of Mawu also have sons of their own, each governing the respective Vodun facets of their fathers, and so the number of Voduns or spirits multiply, each governing specific aspects or facets of life and the world.

Belief in a Soul

Voodoo practitioners believe in the concept of a soul which can leave the body during dreams and spirit possession. In fact, there is an animistic side to Voodoo in which they believe that inanimate objects and natural phenomena such as rocks, trees, storms, etc., possess souls. These souls - whether human or otherwise, comprise the many Loa which are considered spirits, with whom Voodoo practitioners nurture their connection, and through them, with divinity and the spirit world.

Rituals, Priests and Priestesses

The prominence and authority of the Voodoo priests and priestesses stem from their close connection with the spirits, and the honor and respect accorded to ancestors also yield to hereditary lines of priestesses. Thus they are expected to perform many of the affairs for which people go to the spirits in the first place: healing, advice, and various solutions to life's problems. Voodoo priests and priestesses (Juju man or woman) practice an elaborate system of folk medicinal practices, and they also draw on the wisdom and ethical practices of the past through oral traditions of songs, proverbs, stories and folklore, many of which have been passed down through generations upon generations. Needless to say, magic and sorcery - with the aid of the spirits - is also practiced by Voodoo priests and priestesses.

This asking for help is sometimes accompanied by sacrificial offerings of chicken or sheep or the pouring of alcohol. In West Africa, human sacrifices ended almost a century ago, so these days, animals are tradionally sacrificed. There are also festivals or gatherings which are certainly partly or mostly religious in nature, and although the names of these festivals or celebrations and their purposes vary depending on the region and the traditions of the people celebrating them, the essence is the same: spiritual contact with the Voduns, and a recognition and celebration of the Vodun's power over matters on earth.

Talismans and Fetishes

Central to any Voodoo culture is a marketplace that sells talisman ingredients called "fetishes." The uses of these talismans or charms (also called "gris-gris") can vary from medicinal to spiritual powers, and a trip to a fetish market can yield an interesting array of ingredients such as stones, dried animal heads, animal parts, or elaborate statues that represent any of the diverse Voodoo gods. Voodoo shrines can usually be seen topped with various Voodoo fetishes, and these shrines would be placed strategically to protect family homes or areas, and food or wine are laid before these shrines as offerings to the Vodun spirits.

Chapter Three: The Different Strains of Voodoo

Throughout the years, Voodoo has proven itself as lasting and resilient, especially given that its history was closely tied with one of the world's darkest history of human exploitation - the African slave trade. But perhaps because it's because Voodoo has also provided the transplanted slaves with a connection to their old life and their homeland that it endured. Voodoo also offered them a way of defying their European masters, and it kept them strong and the African communities together as it governed not only their religious but also their cultural life.

In this and in the following chapters, we take a closer look at the growth of Voodoo based on the area of its practice. From its home ground of West Africa, to the West

Indies and America's Louisiana, how it had grown distinct to each area, how it figures into the lives of its practitioners, and how it has endured throughout the years.

West African Voodoo

Voodoo was declared an official religion in 1996 in Benin, the country of its origin, and arguably still the center of voodoo in the world - even though it was suppressed and outlawed during Matthew Kerekou's Marxist military rule which ended in 1991. Voodoo certainly began to thrive afterwards, and Benin's annual voodoo festival, a public holiday celebrated each year on January 10 in Ouidah, is considered one of West Africa's most vibrant and colorful events. Tourists come in droves to partake in the celebration of dancing, drinking, music, animal sacrifice and blood offering. But the essence of this religion can easily be missed with all the rich and colorful ceremonies and rituals that also do manifest a dark side - with observances that are strange to many foreigners.

Demographics of Voodoo Faithful in West Africa

These days, there are around 30 million people in the West African nations of Benin, Togo and Ghana that practice Voodoo. Officially, there are also Christians and Muslims in West Africa, but it is notable that many of them practice a syncretized form of their religions, whereby many elements of indigenous African religions - including Voodoo - are incorporated into their practice of Christianity and Islam. But the very adaptability of Voodoo is characteristic of this religion - and in the region of West Africa - Voodoo practices have incorporated many of the elements not just of Christianity and Islam, but also of other indigenous African religions.

Voodoo is actively practiced by certain populations in Ghana, Togo, Benin, Lagos, and Nigeria. All of these scattered peoples who do practice Voodoo are, however, notable for belonging to Gbe-speaking ethnic groups. The Gbe languages comprise some twenty related languages, the five major dialect clusters of which are Ewe, Fon, Aja, Gen and Phla-Phera. These languages are believed to be instrumental in the development of Caribbean creole languages - which would also follow the spread of Voodoo in the West Indies. Interestingly, the Gbe peoples migrated to their present residences in West Africa from the East - which means that Voodoo and many of the other indigenous African relgions may have originated from the interior regions of Africa, though Voodoo has certainly proven itself characteristically distinct, and certainly resilient.

The Spiritual Life of West Africa

Animism figures strongly into the Voodoo practices of West African Voodoo practitioners. Spirits are honored in the forces of nature, in earth elements such as streams, trees, rocks, caves, which are considered powerful and divine. Dead ancestors are also considered spirits or voduns and are considered protectors of their respective clans or tribes.

The divine creator Mawu is female, and she bore seven children who were given power over realms of nature, natural phenomena, and historical and mythical personages. But there is also a male counterpart to Mawu, who is Legba, and their child is Dan, an androgynous serpent that mediates between the living and the spirits or the divine.

As with many traditional religions that see the divine in nature, nature is also considered divine, and thus also powerful. So rituals are formulated incorporating natural ingredients, whether in spells, charms, or herbal remedies.

Priestesses (also called voodooshi) descend from a lineage of clan or tribal priestesses, and they preside over life transitions such as marriages, funerals and baptisms. But priestesses are not exclusive to religious functions - they also occupy a dominant role in communal functions such as the organizations of the market, and in leading the women of the community in prayers and collective worship.

A Voodoo priest or pope (called a voodoonou), is also prominent, especially during celebrations and festivals, as they lead the devoted in offering prayers and sacrifices, as the voodooshi also lead the womenfolk in making their sacrifices and offerings.

Chapter Four: Vodou in the Caribbean

Voodoo in the Caribbean is usually spelled Vodou, sometimes also called Vaudou, or Vodun. The displaced African slaves who were brought to the islands in the Caribbean reinforced their African identity amidst the hardships of slavery, partly through the practice of Vodou. In fact, Vodou in the Caribbean, particularly in Haiti, was instrumental in the African slaves' struggle for freedom.

Caribbean Vodou

The Caribbean is a region in the West Indies comprising several islands and island states and nations that are situated in the Caribbean basin and the North Atlantic Ocean. Voodoo is actively practiced in the islands of Cuba, The Dominican Republic, Haiti, Jamaica, and Puerto Rico. Most especially in Haiti, however, where the common saying now is that Haiti is "70% Catholic, 30% Protestant, and 100% Voodoo."

Needless to say, many of the transplanted slaves from West Africa during the height of Atlantic slave trade were brought to the Caribbean region. Much of the driving force of the Atlantic slave trade, in fact, was Europe's "discovery" of the Americas and the severe shortage of labor as they explored and settled into these new lands. From the 17th to the 19th century, the European countries of France, Britain, Netherlands and Spain subdivided the West Indies among themselves into their respective colonial territories.

After Christopher Columbus discovered the Americas, the Caribbean was a highly contested area among the European powers during the colonial era. Soon after the Spanish crown established its properties in Puerto Rico, Jamaica, Cuba, Trinidad, and Hispaniola (modern Haiti), the native people were enslaved, but forced labor drove them to near extinction. Thus, Spain supplemented the need for labor by importing African slaves. When the Spanish Empire began to decline, the other European powers began establishing their presence in the Caribbean, such as the Dutch, the French, and the British. Just like Spain, they brought African slaves into the region to support the tropical plantation system in the Caribbean.

Millions of slaves were brought into the Caribbean by the British, Dutch, French, Portuguese and Spanish powers via the Atlantic slave trade, and this went on from the 16th to the 19th century. These slaves were forced to work in the plantations, and they lived and worked in inhumane conditions. The separate sale of slaves wrought the destruction of matrimonial and family bonds among the slaves, as they were separated from their spouses and children. Harsh punishment was meted upon them, for attempts to escape, rebellion, theft, and other acts that displeased their masters. But even as their European masters also sought to stamp out the practice of indigenous African religions, many of the slaves disguised their spirits or loa as the Roman Catholic saints.

The actual practice of voodoo, in fact, went underground. But in a sense, the process of sycretism already began to take place, and this was aided by the separation of families and lineages - which also disrupted the passing on of traditional beliefs and religious practices. In seeking to piece together the remnants of what they knew of their African heritage, what resulted was a unique merging of Catholi, native American, and African elements, yielding a unique voodoo practice that has grown beyond its African origins, to produce a uniquely Caribbean style of voodoo.

The overall intolerable conditions in which the African slaves existed caused frequent slave uprisings and rebellions in the region, and Voodoo was an important part of the struggle of the slaves to win their freedom.

Haitian Revolution and the Bois Caiman Ceremony

In 1685, a law was passed in Haiti that required the European masters to Christianize their slaves within eight days of their arrival. The slaves openly accepted Roman Catholicism, but in truth they worshipped by integrating their traditional beliefs under the mask of Roman Catholic elements. Catholic saints were identified with the Voodoo spirits, and Catholic rituals, practices and images were used to conceal what were essentially African religious practices.

It does seem that this open and yet subversive kind of voodoo practice only served to deeply ingrain the practice into the people, as it also strengthened them to fight for their freedom. From 1791 to 1804, the Haitian Revolution took place, and this thirteen-year slave uprising eventually resulted in the liberation of the Haiti from French colonial rule, and the establishment of the first black republic. And it all began with a historical Vodou ceremony - now famously known as the Bois Caiman ceremony of August 1791.

The Bois Caiman Ceremony of August 1791

On the night of Agust 14, 1791, slaves of adjoining plantations in the French colony of Saint-Domingue gathered together in a woody area in northern mountains - a site known as Bois Caiman. They had come together for a secret voodoo ceremony, and were presided over by Dutty Boukman, a slave leader and Vodou priest.

This meeting was shrouded in mystery, and many historical accounts are conflicting. What was known is that it had been a wild and stormy night, and Boukman began the meeting with a prayer that beseeched strength for the their people as they sought liberty. A woman began to dance, possessed of the spirit of Ezili Dantor - a spirit of Haitian Vodou who is also commonly represented by the Black Madonna, sometimes the Lady of Lourdes, of Catholic belief. But for the Vodouns, she was a Loa or Iwa, a spirit of motherhood, the epitome of a warrior-mother, associated with the black creole pig of Haiti, which was her favorite animal sacrifice.

That night at Bois Caiman, the woman possessed by the spirit of Ezili Dantor took knife in hand and cut the throat of a black pig. The participants marked their foreheads with the pig's blood, and "swore to kill all the whites on the island," thus forming a pact to fight for their freedom.

It is a rather unfortunate reality, however, that many conservative Catholics view this event as nothing more than a "pact with the devil" - a view that undoubtedly speaks to the lack of substantial knowledge not only to the inhumane conditions of the slaves, but also to the true essence of Voodoo practice and spirituality.

Demographics of the Voodoo Faithful in the Caribbean

At present, Vodou is practiced not only in Haiti (where it is now a recognized religion), but also in the Dominican Republic, Cuba, some islands in the Bahamas, as well as in the United States, where Haitians have immigrated. Syncretism with the Catholic religion makes an estimate of the true numbers of practitioners in these areas difficult, though many of those who do practice Vodou also practice Catholicism. It is approximated that about 50% of Haiti's population practice Vodou.

It is also notable that Vodou in the Dominican Republic is considerably less stringent than Haitian Vodou, while Cuban Vodou also integrates Indigenous American traditions with those of African and Catholic beliefs and religious practices.

The Spiritual Life of Vodou in the Caribbean

Just like in West Africa, Vodou in the Caribbean is characterized by animism, and a strong belief in the power of the spirits or the Lowa or Iwa, whose powers the faithful invoke and beseech through the offering of animal sacrifices. Nature, and thus cosmic harmony, is considered essential for the practice of Vodou, which is considered fully in sync with natural laws. The practice of it is integrated within people's culture and lifestyles, from life passages to art and music, agriculture, and the healing of illnesses.

In keeping with the syncretized form of this religion, however, many of the celebrations to which the Vodouns participate in are performed in honor of "creolized" Catholic angels and asaints - such as St. Peter and St. Francis of Assissi. They also honor an almighty God - whom the Haitians refer to as Bondye (from the French *Bon Dieu*, or "good God"), but it is the Iwas or the spirits who are more active in the land of the living - and like the African slaves - the spirits also came from their home ground of Africa, traveling underwater to join and protect their descendents in the Caribbean.

There are 21 nations of the Iwa, and they are considered to belong to "families" who share a surname. Three of the more important nations of Iwa are the Rada, the Nago, and the Kongo. Each of the hundreds of Iwas govern specific spheres of life and death, even fertility. They can be either hot or cool, and some are demanding, and even dangerous if angry or upset.

Spirit possession is central to many of the Vodou celebrations, and as the Loas or Iwas take possession of the living, the living become divine. In a way, this is perhaps another form of resistance against slavery - regardless of how badly they are treated, being divine for those brief moments of spirit possession makes them human - more than human, and not the mere workers and slaves that they are being treated as. In fact, this type of practice equalizes people more than any law or statement of equality. Everyone is welcome to a Vodou temple, everyone can celebrate, and anyone can be taken by a spirit and made divine.

Possessed, the spirits can then impart advice, warnings, prophecies, or messages to those of the living. But like in West Africa, these spirits or Loas are similar in many ways to the ancient Greek gods - some are beneficent, but there are others that are also capricious and demanding.

Vodou became an official religion in Haiti in 2003, but it did not happen without a struggle. Catholics and Christians had referred to the Bois Caiman ceremony which prompted the Haiti uprising as a "pact with the devil," and blamed it for all the tragedies that Haiti had suffered since then: an earthquake in 2010, and a subsequent cholera epidemic.

Although the political manipulation employed by former Haiti president Francois Duvalier (Papa Doc) - who posed as a Vodou priest with supernatural powers - and his organization of Vodou priests in a Reign of Terror, did serve to elevate Vodou into a national doctrine. All these things may have helped to turn many Haitians against the practice of Vodou, and there are those who hate Vodou just as strongly as there are those who live Vodou in their hearts.

Chapter Five: Louisiana Voodoo

Some of the slaves captured on the West African coast were also brought to New Orleans in Louisiana, in the southern part of the United States. Louisiana had also been occupied by various populations including the native Americans, French, Spanish, Germans, Acadians, Creoles, and with the arrival of the Africans, it has been one of the most culturally rich and diverse environment in the United States. Voodoo, which was brought by the uprooted African slaves from their native homeland, thus developed in unique ways which distinguishes it from Haitian and West African Voodoo.

Louisiana Voodoo

Many of the slaves that were brought to the French colony in Louisiana, particularly Southern Louisiana, were able to stay together in large groups, thus enabling them to preserve their culture and practices. And because the French masters - at least nominally - recognized family groups and prohibited the sale of children younger than fourteen years old if this separated them from their families, the slave community in Southern Louisiana was well-integrated, autonomous, functional, and self-confident.

Perhaps because of the comparative leniency of the European masters in Louisiana, Voodoo was not as strong a mobilizing force in Louisiana as it was in Haiti. The French were expelled from Haiti after the succesful revolution of the Haitian slaves, and they came to Louisiana, bringing with them some of their African slaves. Arguably, the arrival of the Haitians breathed new life into the practice of Voodoo, and many of the Voodoo leaders who became prominent in Louisiana came from Haiti or were of Haitian descent.

The African groups that were brought to Louisiana brought with them their knowledge of charms and amulets, as well as herbs and poisons, and these became standard elements of Louisiana Voodoo. Slaves would make and wear charms for either healing or protection, and they were also wary of charms that were used to hurt or poison enemies. Much like in the Caribbean states, Louisiana Voodoo soon developed from a syncretization with the local Catholic religion, and Christian elements such as the invocation of Jehovah, the use of holy candles and incense, holy bread, and crucifixes, and holy water, soon became part of Voodoo rituals.

Voodoo "queens" were widely recognized as having high authority in the community, and this was prevalent among both the slaves and even among the white masters. They made a living selling spells, charms, amulets, magical powders, or other magical tools of Voodoo practice, and it seems that a certain sense of supersition prevailed in the entire community because no one contested their powers. Ceremonial meetings and dances drew hundreds and thousands, and the authority of these voodoo queens were incontestable.

Among these Voodoo queens, and known as the "most powerful of them all," was Marie Laveau. She consulted for everyone - even white businessmen, lawyers and politicians, but she had a particular compassion for the less fortunate. She was also a Catholic, and encouraged many of the African slaves to attend mass, thus in her own way promoting the syncretization of Voodoo with Catholicism, though her intentions may have simply been to help her followers protect their true beliefs by hiding it under the mask of Catholicism. It is said that she worked for a time as a hairdresser, and in this way learning local secrets and gossip in order to support her divinations. She held elaborate public rituals on St. John's Eve at Bayou St. John, drawing in hundreds of thousands of devotees, and her influence and authority as a Voodoo queen was accepted and respected by all.

Perhaps one of the best legacies of Marie Laveau to Voodoo is drawing together black and white races in a recognition of the beauty, the power and the mystery of Voodoo. To this day, Marie Laveau is considered one of the most iconic spiritual leaders in Louisiana: her grave is a major tourist attraction, and it seems that she has entered the ranks of the spirits that Voodoo practitioners invoke for their powers. Offerings are left for Marie Laveau, just as her name is invoked by the superstitious for good fortune, protection, and guidance.

Since the 21st century, Voodoo has become mostly a commercial attraction in New Orleans, Louisiana. A 1932 film "White Zombie" started the typical sensationalist view in popular culture of Voodoo as a dark and dangerous magical practice that involved hexing and cursing. Since then, this perspective on Voodoo has only been solidified by businesses in Louisiana that made their profit by selling

Voodoo trinkets, charms, amulets and "gris-gris." It has also been used as a selling point in tourism- and museums, historical sites, spiritual services, and markets selling Voodoo trinkets and ornaments cater to the interested tourists who are attracted to and curious about the dark and sensational Voodoo in Louisiana.

Perhaps this very interest in the sensational side of Voodoo and many of the other indigenous African religions led to the development of Hoodoo, an offshoot of Voodoo, but with a greater emphasis on folk magic and sorcery.

Demographics of Voodoo Faithful in Louisiana

Despite the strong element of Voodoo in the tourism industry of New Orleans and Louisiana, the true adherents and serious practitioners of Voodoo are, in reality, very few. These days, it is estimated that only about 15% of the population of New Orleans practice Voodoo, though perhaps this does not take into account the various Voodoo-rooted beliefs and superstitions that many in the population adhere to or believe, nor the Voodoo-influenced spiritual systems or churches that still survive in New Orleans. There is a very real danger, though, of Voodoo in New Orleans and Louisiana being absorbed and completely taken in by business and tourism concerns - a far cry from the animist, nature and spirit worship that were the essence of Voodoo's West African origins.

The Spiritual Life of Louisiana Voodoo

It is said that modern Voodoo in Louisiana has developed in diverse directions: there are churches headed by spiritual reverends or mothers; Hoodoo practitioners who make a living from spell working; and there are the traditionalists who practice Voodoo as it was once practiced: as an important part of daily life, a natural connection with the earth and spiritual wisdom, and a positive association with their African roots. Louisiana Voodoo now is basically inseparable from the Afro-Caribbean Roman Catholic influences of its past and the Christian influences in its environment, thus African gods and spirits coexist quite well with Catholic saints, angels, prayers and liturgical worship.

While honor and veneration of spirits, nature and ancestors are the root of all Voodoo religious strains, it does seem that the practice of Voodoo in Louisiana thrives more on its "public face." The accoutrements of Voodoo are highly sought after - talismans, charms, amulets and the popular "gris-gris" are sold commercially, and are actually a means of livelihood for the practicing Voodoo priests and priestesses. Voodoo rituals, on the other hand, are highly embellished, and singing, dancing and the unique blending of harmonics using drums, ceremonial music and instruments, clapping, and feet stomping are utilized widely.

Songs are used to signify the various phases of a ritual - from preparation, invocation, possession, and farewell. Spirit possession is thus also part of Louisiana Voodoo culture, though it seems to be taken as a matter of course. There are, however, "true rituals" conducted behind closed doors - disdaining public showing as disrespectful to the spirits. These rituals are used to heal ailments and to conduct divinatory readings for the Voodoo faithful, and they make use of spiritual baths, readings, diets, prayers, and ceremonies.

Chapter Six: The Dark Side of Voodoo

For a religion that was so instrumental in forming an identity for the African slaves in Haiti, and which has been so instrumental in winning the first African slave revolution, why has Voodoo since then been sensationalized and imprinted upon the public mind as something dark, sinister, and dangerous?

It cannot be denied, however, that Voodoo does have a dark side. Though perhaps not so different from the dark side of Christianity and Catholicism in their depictions of hell, demons, and the devil; it may be said that the dark side of any religion only serves to emphasize the good in the world, much as darkness helps to emphasize the light. It can help us to remember, however, in our study of this religion, that Voodoo came into the world consciousness only with the emergence of African slavery.

Those were almost three centuries and more of oppression, subjugation, humiliation, and tyranny over the African slaves - surely a dark time in African history, and when they cannot openly fight against their oppressors, a more subtle and mystical form of resistance were perhaps their only options. A person who cannot take up arms against his better-equipped oppressors for fear of violent retaliation must take some form of comfort in a manner of secret attack - even if it were through curses or hexes. In the same way, an enslaved man treated no better than an animal resists in his own way during a voodoo ritual when he is possessed by a spirit and thus becomes, even for that short duration, divine.

Any discussion about Voodoo is not complete without a look at the more sensational - though according to some traditional practitioners, considerably rare in actual practice - aspects of Voodoo. In this chapter, we take a look at the elements of Voodoo that have certainly imprinted themselves upon the public mind as well as popular culture.

Curses, Poisons and Hexes

Curses and hexes are an essential part of Voodoo, just as the Voodoo doctors who recognize those curses and hexes and prescribe certain spells or counter-curses to safeguard them from the evil of the spiritual curse or spiritual poison.

Many times, these kinds of curses or poisons are cast because of the baser sides of humanity: greed, revenge, or sheer hatred. The ingredients for both the hex or the curse varies, depending on what are prescribed by the Voodoo practitioner, and on what ingredients are locally available. To help their efficacy, natural phenomena are also integrated: a full moon, the site of a graveyard, streams, rocks, or natural groves. When the curse or the hex manifests itself, the signs usually perplex doctors or other medical practitioners, and only a Voodoo doctor can recognize it as a spiritual poison infecting a person due to a hex or a curse that has been placed upon them.

Whether or not these things are true or factual reality cannot be said - it really depends on the point of view of a person, and their spiritual beliefs. Though perhaps what cannot be denied is that there are those who do believe in these things, and they do cast curses or hexes against their enemies, just as there are those who also believe who seek spiritual help from Voodoo practitioners.

Voodoo Dolls

Voodoo dolls are effigies of real persons, and the theory is that with the use of tangible personal items from the real person being represented, a link is formed between doll and person so that anything done to the doll also happens to the person. Historically, however, Voodoo dolls were used by African wise men to communicate with the Loa, or the spirits whom they revere - whenever they seek guidance or help. When the African slaves traversed the ocean to come to America under conditions of indentured servitude, many of their traditional religious beliefs and practices became fragmented and the original purposes diffused. Thus, Voodoo dolls began to be used for a variety of different purposes.

But the use of dolls are not exclusive to Voodoo, and neither are they prominent in traditional Voodoo practice. Perhaps it was mostly due to the influence of film and media that the use of dolls in black magic or dark sorcery have been popularly referred to as Voodoo dolls, thus reinforcing public perceptions of Voodoo as something evil.

These days, however, the sinister little Voodoo doll with the pins sticking out of them has certainly evolved - they are now made available commercially, and are used as much for positive magical workings as for nefarious intentions. Those versed in alternative spiritual systems will be quick to say that in magic and sorcery, intent is always the determining factor in everything, and it is perhaps true that even in Voodoo magic, positive intentions can be just as true as negative ones. The Voodoo doll then is not evil per se - what it is, is merely a tool for intent.

Zombies

There are many possible derivations of the English word "zombie," including Haitian Creole *zonbi*, Haitian French *zombi*, Kongo *nzambi* (meaning god) or *zumbi* (fetish). In essence, however, zombies are popularly known to be corpses of dead persons reanimated or brought back to life through magical means.

The use of the trope "walking undead" has certainly evolved over the years in literature and media, but the original introduction of the concept to the western world was through the book *"The Magic Island"* by W.B. Seabrook, detailing a fictionalized account of the narrator's encounter with voodoo cults and zombies in Haiti. And in the years 1915 to 1934, during the USA's occupation of Haiti, American soldiers brought back with them tales of black magic and walking dead. Since then, zombies have certainly fed into the rich imaginations of the western world, until they are now virtually unrecognizable from that of the Voodoo zombies of Haitian folklore.

The ironic thing is that zombies, or the belief in zombies, actually do not play a part in Voodoo religous practices or rituals, nor in Voodoo spiritual beliefs. In Voodoo, the dead are revered and honored, and those who have passed on are considered spirits or Loas with whom the living interact and ask for guidance, help or protection. This contrasts with the natural terror or fear that will certainly be inspired by the sight of a dead corpse walking the earth as though it were still alive.

Perhaps the closest connection that zombies can have to Voodoo religious practice is the essential spirit possession that characterizes much of Voodoo rituals. When a spirit or a Loa possesses a practitioner, they are, if only for a brief moment, walking the earth. The belief is that the dead and the living coexist on this earth, but while the extraordinary powers of the dead are respected (it is believed that touching a person possessed by a dead ancestor or spirit is enough to cause a person's death), neither are they feared in the same way as the zombie's of popular culture.

On the other hand, there does seem to be some obscure traditional Vodou account for zombies. It is said that people who die an unnatural death - due to murder or the like - are unable to rest, and so they will linger near their graves. Well-meaning Bokors (Voodoo priests) may snatch their souls and sealed in a bottle, and either their soul or their body are utilized by the Bokor. Sometimes, the dead person himself might prefer to work rather than to just lie underground, waiting, and the assistance of a zombie can be beneficial in magical works of healing. Although there are also unsavory Bokos who will target the living to make a zombie whom then can thereafter enslave.

Allegedly, there are different ways by which a zombie might be restored: the death of the Bokor will release their hold on the zombie, feeding salt to a zombie will reverse the effects of their death-like trance, or through the divine intervention of a Voodoo god called Le Grand Maitre.

It is interesting to note, however, that some traditional South African beliefs do recognize zombies - as dead corpses brought back to life through witchcraft, and who are then enslaved by the witch to do her bidding. Other accounts claim that the witch "zombifies" a living person, thereby taking over their will completely until they are enslaved by the witch. Remarkably, a Harvard ethnobiologist named Wade Davis presented a pharmacological explanation for the zombies in Haiti.

According to Davis, special powders and chemical compounds, or neuro-muscular toxins, can be used to induce a death-like state in a person, after which the victim's will is completely subjected to that of the caster - or a Voodoo priest that is called a "Bokor" in Haiti. Re-animation takes place after burial, in which instance the zombie realizes their identity as someone who was already dead. What brings these historical trivia full circle is the fact that William Seabrook's "The Magic Island" was written after he read the Haitian Criminal Code which punished as murder the employment of substances which produces a lethargic coma, "without causing actual death." The provision goes on to say: "If, after the administering of such substances, the person has been buried, the act shall be considered murder no matter what result follows." Writer and anthropologist Zora Neale Hurston is of the opinion that much of Voodoo sorcery might actually be traceable to a unique and penetrating knowledge of the properties of herbs, plants, and other natural substances - making Voodoo knowledge of medicine and, in contrast, poisons - certainly formidable.

These days, zombies have evolved in popular culture to the extent that their links to Voodoo practice has all but been forgotten - and they grace various media as cartoons, games, and post-apocalyptic films as walking dead hungering for living flesh. But while tales of monsters all over the world includes one form of another of walking dead, what does seem to be certain is that in Haiti, there have been long-ago accounts of relatives who have died and been buried and were thereafter seen by their living family walking about as though they were still alive, of witch trains manned by zombies, or of plantations whose work was being carried out by subject zombies.

Are zombies real, then? Many are skeptical, and so zombies have not really been taken seriously enough to warrant close investigation. Wade Davis's pharmacological explanation has been criticized enough by experts who scoff at the plausibility of drugs working to the extent that a person can remain in a deathlike trance for years, while still being able to move around. Without further investigation, however, widespread accounts of zombies in Haiti can only remain nothing more than speculation and superstition. Many modern Voodoo practitioners elsewhere certainly do not recognize zombies as part of their religion.

Juju and Hoodoo

Juju is essentially a magical concept, and is often used to refer to magical talismans, charms, or fetishes employed in many indigenous African religions, including Voodoo. The word derives from West African origin, akin to Hausa djudju, which are used to refer to fetishes. In Yoruban terms, however, Ju-Ju refers to a native music or dance form that is characterized by rapid beats, percussion instruments, and vocal harmonies.

Over the years, however, popular usage has more often than not used the term juju to refer to anything magical, whether a charm or talisman, to the powers of the one casting the spell, or the luck of a person who has fallen afoul of magical workings. Thus, "It's bad juju" or "The person can look at you and give you bad juju." Interestingly, the term is no longer exclusive to dark or evil workings. Some usages also include positive magical workings, or "good juju." Once again, it seems apparent that - similar to many neopagan and alternative spiritualities, intent is a determining factor in whether magic, or a magical instrument, is considered good or evil. But with the increasing commercialization of the religion of Voodoo, these days, there are magical workers called marabouts who are ply their trade by the crafting and selling of juju items.

On the other hand, Hoodoo is an offshoot of Voodoo and other indigenous African Religions - mainly Central African traditional beliefs, but many Voodoo practitioners take pains to point out that despite common origins and a seeming similarity in word usage, Hoodoo is not the same as Voodoo, even despite the seeming interchangeability of the two words. It is probably more appropriate to view Hoodoo as akin to traditional notions of witchcraft, especially since the word itself only came into use after Voodoo and other African religions began to evolve in the Americas, integrating native American and even European myths, folklore and superstitions.

Otherwise also associated with conjurings, witchcraft, rootwork, candle burning, or tricking, Hoodoo is witchcraft and sorcery essentially, though the elements used and its associations are African in origin. These days, Hoodoo can be used to refer to an entire system of magical practices and rituals, where curses, bad luck and ghosts are only a small portion of the whole, and can either be healing or harmful in its practice. In a sense, the term can be used intechangeably with "witchcraft" or "bewitching," (i.e., "I've been hoodooed," or "I've been bewitched."), and Hoodoo practices as conjurings or spell casting, where the practitioner is usually referred to as a "root-worker" or a Hoodoo doctor or Hoodoo woman.

But as in most spiritual systems where what people know are based more on imaginative conjectures rather than actual knowledge, Hoodoo has been touched with negative connotations, and some people inevitably associated it with harmful curses or spells, jinxes and curses, though in some instances, it also includes curative magic to counter these spells, jinxes and curses. In a way, this does touch on the essential difference between Hoodoo and Voodoo: Voodoo is a religion that works with venerated spirits who can intervene in human life and bestow wisdom or protection.

Hoodoo, on the other hand, emphasizes magical powers and their practical use or application in life.

But aside from the seeming similarity of the two terms Hoodoo and Voodoo, another commonality that these two spiritual systems also share is a history of syncretization with Catholicism which the slaves were forced to adopt, as well as being a subtle outlet for the transplanted African slaves to fight back in some of the only ways they can, given their horrendous conditions. Thus, Hoodoo spells were employed to give a person healing and protection, and to cast harm upon their enemies. As with many other spiritual systems that integrate magic into their belief systems, intent is always considered decisive, and Hoodoo elements essentially neutral without the active intent of the caster.

Chapter Seven: Voodoo and Racism

As we have seen from the previous chapters, Voodoo is essentially an African-rooted religion that celebrates their beliefs in spirits, their connection with nature, and a deep veneration and honor for their ancestors. But because of the sensational and selective portrayal of Voodoo in popular culture, to the uninformed, the term Voodoo usually conjures images of dark and sinister forces where voodoo dolls and zombies are central to shadowy and evil magic. Many who hold these perspectives are often of the opinion that Voodoo is nothing more than ignorant superstition, a delusion of the uneducated, and certainly inferior to the major religions such as Christianity. But is it accurate to say that these prejudices against Voodoo are also a symptom of persisting racism against the once-denigrated slave race?

Catholic and Christian Prejudices

There is a long history of the dominance of the Catholic-Christian church, and what its effects had been on the more traditional, pagan, and nature-based religions the world over. Voodoo is certainly not the sole recipient of Catholic biases against anything that is different from itself. In a way, this cannot be helped by Christian doctrine - they believe in a single, Almighty God, and a one true religion. Therefore, anything that does not fall into or adhere to Christian doctrine or religion is considered invalid - or worse, labeled as evil, or as the contraindication of the goodness of the Almighty God (i.e., the work of the devil).

These are what Christians believe, just as Voodoo practitioners believe in the power of spirits. And where belief is strong on each side, and is not founded on anything more substantial or concrete other than faith, arguments are likely to go on ad infinitum ad nauseaum. Recently, Christian evangelicals have controversially touted Voodoo ceremonies as a pact with devil, accounting therefore for the disasters and tragedies that befell Haiti - one of the countries with a rich practice of Voodoo. But the concept of the devil is exclusive to Christian beliefs, while Voodoo indubitably precedes Christianity and Catholicism, and perhaps most of the religions currently practiced on earth. To them, what is considered evil or works of the devil by outsiders is divine or spiritual, and that includes many of the more showy aspects of Voodoo - such as animal sacrifices, ritual dancing, and spirit possession. Human nature often looks at what is strange and unfamiliar through the eyes of fear, and many misconceptions are formed which can easily be displaced by proper information and an open and nonjudgmental mind.

Ignorance, Fear, and Racism

The connection between pop culture's images of Voodoo and racism are obvious enough to students of history, though in this author's opinion, not studied or acknowledged enough. The Europeans made slaves of a race which they considered inferior, uneducated, ignorant, and savage, thus also seeing them as incapable and unworthy of enjoying many of the universal human values such as familial relationships, the capacity and right to be educated, the right to proper living conditions, the right to self-governance, and of course, the right to worship as they please. And this was true not only for the African slave race, but also for many indigenous peoples and lands all over the world which the European powers had occupied during the 18th century in the race for world domination. From the other side of the coin, however, it might be interesting to

consider that the Europeans powers were actually the cause
and catalyst of the ills and troubles they identified in the
peoples they conquered and enslaved.

Necessarily, anything indigenous or native - such as their
forms of worship, were also considered inferior, and thus
prohibited. The local forms of worship were inferior and
rooted in ignorance, and were thus portrayed appropriately:
cannibalism, wild dances and sexual orgies, devil worship,
and black magic. These are tales of horror that have
captured the imaginations of sensationalist filmmakers, and
in the eventual portrayal of Voodoo in the mass film
industry as something that invokes horror and terror, public
perception follows a close and direct link with the original
prejudices that European colonialists held against their
African slaves. Yes, there is a deep-rooted racism and even
bigotry at the heart of most pop culture perceptions on
Voodoo. And though it is also important to remember that
the film industry caters more to entertainment than to
education, it has indirectly but indelibly contributed to the
current prevalence of many of the misconceptions regarding
Voodoo in the public mind. The very dismissiveness that
many people have against its legitimacy as a real religion
also dismisses the reality that for many of the African slaves
and their descendants, Voodoo has given them the spiritual
strength to fight for their freedom and for their worth as
individuals and as a nation.

The best weapon against ignorance and fear, they say, is education and an open mind. Thankfully, these days, many anthropologists, historians, and even field reporters, are delving into Voodoo as a valid and ancient spiritual system. The Catholic Church, under Pope John Paul II, has openly spoken of the esteem that he holds for Voodoo and its practitioners, and the recognition of Voodoo as a valid religion in the state of Benin is certainly a win for authentic African culture, and practicing it openly and freely, where many foreigners and tourists are also invited to take part, can only serve to assist in breaking centuries of racial prejudice and historical enmity.

Chapter Eight: Voodoo Myths and Facts

In this book, we have learned a lot about Voodoo as a spiritual system, its history and its dissemination throughout the world, and how it has evolved through contact with other religious systems. Perhaps one of the most important things we have learned is how little people actually know of this religion. In this final chapter, we take a brief look at some of the more salient points regarding Voodoo, under the opposing headings of Myths and Facts.

Voodoo Myths

- *That Voodoo dolls are evil.* Many Voodoo dolls are actually used for benevolent purposes. Historically, they were used by African priests and spiritual leaders to communicate with the spirits of their deceased ancestors for wisdom and guidance. It all depends on the intentions of the person using it. But overall, the use of Voodoo dolls are not prominent or central to Voodoo religious beliefs.

- *That Voodoo is used to harm or cause injury and mischief.* While there are certain darker facets of Voodoo practices, it all depends on the practitioner. These days, many of the faithful use Voodoo more for healing, for seeking guidance and wisdom in their daily lives, and have openly disavowed the more nefarious uses of Voodoo spiritual practice.

- *That Voodoo is about black magic, curses, hexes, poisons, voodoo dolls and zombies.* This view of Voodoo is essentially a Western creation - and feeds largely into the public's interest into the strange, the frightening, the dark and the unnatural. Given that this perception is essentially created by people outside of Voodoo, those who have no true understanding of the essential spiritual beliefs that the Voodoo faithful adhere to, and are largely promulgated to cater either to commercial interests in "selling Voodoo," this really should not be taken seriously. While there is a "dark side" to Voodoo, this is hardly central to their practices and beliefs - which are more about the celebration of life and our connection with the spirits and the divine, of healing, of communal relationships, and spiritual tranformation.

- *That the Haitian Earthquake was caused by its Vodou heritage and is a punishment by God.* There is no truth to an earthquake being caused by one's religious beliefs, or as punishment for them - earthquakes happen in many countries all over the world, and their effects devastate everybody, regardless of class or culture. Vodou, on the other hand, is a long legacy of philosophies, ancient wisdom, cosmology, language, medical therapies, rites of passage, codes of conduct, artistic conventions, and aesthetic norms that provide entire communities with a shared sense of identity. There is nothing in Vodou that deserves punishment.

Voodoo Facts

- The precise origins or the founders of Voodoo are unknown, but Voodoo is considered to be an ancient spiritual system that is perhaps as old as humanity itself. The word Voodoo actually stands for "spirit" or "Great Spirit" - which is a central concept in Voodoo beliefs and cosmology.
- In the Americas, the West African slaves were required to adopt Christianity and Catholicism as a religion, so the practice of Voodoo evolved into a

syncretized form of Catholicism, indigenous African religious practices, and even native American traditional practices. In a very real sense, Voodoo is an inclusive religion, adaptable and capable of evolving with the times.

- The snake has a prominent place in Voodoo lore, as the serpent god Damballa, the creator of the world and the protector of the young and helpless. He transports the souls of the dead to the afterlife, and is commonly venerated as one of the oldest among the Voodoo pantheon.

- Voodoo honors and venerates the spirits of their ancestors and the spirits in nature, especially the snake who is considered one of the oldest of the Loas or spirits that watch over humanity,

- The use of animal sacrifice in many Voodoo rituals and ceremonies is rooted in the belief of a life force that reportedly runs through the offering of blood, a worthy offering that can rejuvenate the life force of the spirit invoked.

- Marie Laveau was a prominent and iconic Voodoo queen in Louisiana, and she was instrumental in spreading the power and influence of Voodoo beliefs, practices and rituals among the population, both among the slaves and the European masters. To this day, her name and influence holds particular sway among the Louisiana population, and her wisdom, guidance and blessings are still invoked by many.

- The Catholic Church recognizes the legitimacy of Voodoo, and in 1993, even Pope John Paul II has spoken of the fundamental goodness inherent in the practices, teachings and beliefs of Voodoo.

- While there is a dark side to Voodoo - it is not very prominent among the actual practitioners. Voodoo itself, in essence is not a "dark" religion - it honors nature, life, and the connections between the visible and the invisible world.

- Voodoo is what the people make it. It is largely an oral tradition passed down through generations through songs, ceremonies, folklore, stories, music and dance. It is not a dogmatic form of worship that derives its ethics from a standard set of codified rules. Neither is it good or bad. It is what the people make it - and over the years, the people have made it, and proven, that Voodoo is adaptable, resilient, empowering, rich and colorful, and inclusive of those who believe something different, and of those who are the lowly or the downtrodden in society. Everyone is essentially equal. Voodoo is also about harmony with nature and the spirits, a belief in one Supreme Being, honor for one's ancestors, and the importance of a functional and responsive community and communal relations. It is about the way we treat our family, friends, neighbors, enemies, our past, and the environment around us. In essence, Voodoo is a way of life more than simply a form of religion.

Index

A

Agbe	15
Agê	15
ancestor worship	13, 62
animal sacrifice	62
animism	13, 62

B

Belief in a Divine Creator	5, 12
Belief in a Soul	5, 16
Bois Caiman Ceremony	27

C

Caribbean Vodou	23
Catholicism and Christianity	54, 63
Curses, Poisons and Hexes	43

D

dark side of voodoo	41, 43, 63
Demographics of the Voodoo Faithful in the Caribbean	28
Demographics of Voodoo Faithful in Louisiana	37
Demographics of Voodoo Faithful in West Africa	20
different strains of voodoo	19

E

elements of voodoo	11, 12

G

Gu   15

H

Haitian Revolution and the Bois Caiman Ceremony   26
History of Voodoo   5, 6, 73
hoodoo   37, 49

I

Ignorance, Fear, and Racism   6, 55
Dominican Republic   28

J

Jo   15
Juju   49

L

Louisiana Voodoo   6, 33, 34, 35, 38, 39, 74, 76

N

nature worship   22

P

priests and priestesses   16, 22

R

racism   53

Rituals   16, 22

S

Sakpata   15

slavery   26

sons of Mawu   16

Spiritual Life of Louisiana Voodoo   38

Spiritual Life of Vodou in the Caribbean   29

Spiritual Life of West Africa   21

supreme being   12

T

Talismans and Fetishes   5, 17

V

Vodoo   5

Voodoo Spirits   5, 13

Voodoo Dolls   44, 75

Voodoo Facts   59, 61

Voodoo Myths   59

W

West African Voodoo   5, 20, 21, 34, 77

What is Voodoo   5

X

Xêvioso (or Xêbioso)   15

Z

Zombies   6, 2, 45, 74, 77, 79

Photo Credits

Page 1 Photo by Greg Willis, as uploaded by Infrogmation via Wikimedia Commons.
<https://commons.wikimedia.org/wiki/File:Voodoo_Altar_New_Orleans.jpg>

Page 5 Photo by Afrikit via Pixabay.
<https://pixabay.com/en/voodoo-dance-benin-traditional-736095/>

Page 11 Photo by jbdodane via Wikimedia Commons.
<https://commons.wikimedia.org/wiki/File:Voodoo_Market_Bohicon_(Benin).jpg>

Page 19 by Dominik Schwarz via Wikimedia Commons.
<https://commons.wikimedia.org/wiki/File:Voodo-altar.jpg>

Page 23 Photo by Jeremy Burgin via Wikimedia Commons.
<https://commons.wikimedia.org/wiki/File:Voodoo_altar_in_Tropenmuseum.jpg>

Page 33 Photo by ciamabue via Wikimedia Commons.
<https://commons.wikimedia.org/wiki/File:VoodooSpirtualTempleNOLAAug05.jpg>

Page 41 Photo by JNL (Jean-noël Lafargue) delinavit et uploadit) via Wikimedia Commons.
<https://commons.wikimedia.org/wiki/File:Zombie_haiti_ill_artlibre_jnl.png>

Page 53 Photo by Ar7495 via Pixabay.
<https://pixabay.com/en/slave-family-statue-heritage-706721/>

Page 59 Photo by mexolive via Pixabay.
<https://pixabay.com/en/slave-castle-elmina-ghana-947762/>

References

"10 Things You Didn't Know About Voodoo." Debra Kelly. <http://listverse.com/2013/12/11/10-things-you-didnt-know-about-voodoo/>

"A Brief History of Voodoo." New Orleans Voodoo Crossroads. <http://www.neworleansvoodoocrossroads.com/historyandvoodoo.html>

"Africa." Wikipedia. <https://en.wikipedia.org/wiki/Africa>

"African diaspora." Wikipedia. <https://en.wikipedia.org/wiki/African_diaspora>

"Atlantic Slave Trade." Wikipedia. <https://en.wikipedia.org/wiki/Atlantic_slave_trade>

"Benin." Wikipedia. <https://en.wikipedia.org/wiki/Benin>

"Black Magic: Hoodoo Witches Speak Out on the Appropriation of Their Craft." Gabby Bess. <https://broadly.vice.com/en_us/article/black-magic-talking-with-hoodoo-witches>

"Bois Caïman." Wikipedia. <https://en.wikipedia.org/wiki/Bois_Ca%C3%AFman>

"Cannibals and Savages: Racism and images of Haiti." David Schmidt.

<https://canadiandimension.com/articles/view/cannibals-and-savages>

"Cuban Vudú." Wikipedia.
<https://en.wikipedia.org/wiki/Cuban_Vod%C3%BA>

"Dominican Vudú." Wikipedia.
<https://en.wikipedia.org/wiki/Dominican_Vud%C3%BA>

"Ezili Dantor." Wikipedia.
<https://en.wikipedia.org/wiki/Ezili_Dantor>

"From Benin to Bourbon Street: A Brief History of Louisiana Voodoo." Kim Kelly. <http://noisey.vice.com/blog/from-benin-to-bourbon-street-a-brief-history-of-louisiana-voodoo>

"Gbe languages." Wikipedia.
<https://en.wikipedia.org/wiki/Gbe_languages>

"Haiti & The Truth About Zombies." umich.edu.
<http://www.umich.edu/~uncanny/zombies.html>

"Haiti: Possessed by Voodoo." Sharon Guynup.
<http://news.nationalgeographic.com/news/2004/07/0707_04
0707_tvtaboovoodoo.html>

"Haitian Vodou." haitianconsulate.org.
<http://www.haitianconsulate.org/vodou.html>

"Haitian Vodou." Wikipedia.
<https://en.wikipedia.org/wiki/Haitian_Vodou>

"History of the Caribbean." Wikipedia.
<https://en.wikipedia.org/wiki/History_of_the_Caribbean>:

"Hoodoo, Conjure, and Rootwork: African American Folk Magic." Catherine Yronwode.
<http://www.luckymojo.com/hoodoohistory.html>

"Hoodoo (Folk Magic)." Wikipedia.
<https://en.wikipedia.org/wiki/Hoodoo_(folk_magic)>

"How Do Voodoo Dolls Actually Work?" Botanica.
<https://www.originalbotanica.com/blog/voodoo-dolls-rituals-spells/>

"How Voodoo Works." Tracy V. Wilson.
<http://people.howstuffworks.com/voodoo.htm>

"Juju." Your Dictionary.
<http://www.yourdictionary.com/juju>

"Juju: Definition." Merriam Webster. <http://www.merriam-webster.com/dictionary/juju>

"Juju." Wikipedia. <https://en.wikipedia.org/wiki/Juju>

"Juju, the dark side of Voodoo." Black Magic World.com.
<http://blackmagicworld.com/juju-the-dark-side-of-voodoo.html>

"Louisiana." Wikipedia.
<https://en.wikipedia.org/wiki/Louisiana>

"Louisiana Voodoo." Wikipedia.
<https://en.wikipedia.org/wiki/Louisiana_Voodoo>

"Marie Laveau." Wikipedia.
<https://en.wikipedia.org/wiki/Marie_Laveau>

"Myths Obscure Voodoo, Source of Comfort in Haiti."
Samuel G. Freedman.
<http://www.nytimes.com/2010/02/20/world/americas/20reli
gion.html?_r=0>

"Myths of Voodoo, Spirits, and Black Magic." Fractal
Enlightenment.
<http://fractalenlightenment.com/32009/culture/myths-of-
voodoo-spirits-and-black-magic>

"New Orleans." Wikipedia.
<https://en.wikipedia.org/wiki/New_Orleans#Religion>

"New Orleans Voodoo's African Origins." New Orleans
Official Guide.
<http://www.neworleansonline.com/neworleans/multicultur
al/multiculturaltraditions/voodoo.html>

"Ritual dance, goat slaughtering and gin: Thousands gather
for voodoo religious festival in tinyy African country of
Benin." James Dunn.
<http://www.dailymail.co.uk/news/article-3393417/Ritual-
dances-goat-slaughtering-gin-Thousands-gather-Voodoo-
religious-festival-tiny-African-country-Benin.html>

"Shedding Light on Voodoo Rituals in Haiti." David Rosenberg. <http://www.slate.com/blogs/behold/2013/11/06/anthony_karen_a_photographer_s_look_inside_a_haitian_voodoo_ritual_photos.html>

"Spirits, Shrines and Spells: The Story of West African Voodoo." <James Bainbridge. https://afktravel.com/99746/the-story-of-west-african-voodoo/>

"The Gods of the Caribbean." Voodou Mythology. <http://www.godchecker.com/pantheon/caribbean-mythology.php>

"The Mysterious Real Zombies of Haiti." Brent Swancer. <http://www.umich.edu/~uncanny/zombies.html >

"The Myth of "Voodoo": A Caribbean American Response to Representations of Haiti." Dianne Diakite. <http://religiondispatches.org/the-myth-of-voodoo-a-caribbean-american-response-to-representations-of-haiti/>

"The Origins of Voodoo, the Misunderstood Religion." Ancient Origins. <http://www.ancient-origins.net/history-ancient-traditions/origins-voodoo-misunderstood-religion-002933?nopaging=1>

"The Reality of Voodoo in Benin." BBC News. <http://www.bbc.com/news/world-africa-15792001>

"Traditional African religion." Wikipedia.
<https://en.wikipedia.org/wiki/Traditional_African_religion>

"Vodou is elusive and endangered, but it remains the soul of
Haitian people." Kim Wall and Caterina Clerici.
<https://www.theguardian.com/world/2015/nov/07/vodou-
haiti-endangered-faith-soul-of-haitian-people>

"Voodoo." African Holocaust.
<http://www.africanholocaust.net/news_ah/vodoo.htm>

"Voodoo." Frommer's.
<http://www.frommers.com/destinations/new-
orleans/717241>

"Voodoo a Legitimate Religion, Anthropologist Says." Brian
Handwerk for National Geographic News.
<http://news.nationalgeographic.com/news/2002/10/1021_02
1021_taboovoodoo.html>

"Voodoo: A Religion Born in Africa." afrotourism.com.
<http://afrotourism.com/travelogue/voodoo-a-religion-born-
in-africa/>

"Voodoo and West Africa's Spiritual Life." John Burnett.
<http://www.npr.org/templates/story/story.php?storyId=166
6721>

"Voodoo Doll." Wikipedia.
<https://en.wikipedia.org/wiki/Voodoo_doll>

Feeding Baby
Cynthia Cherry
978-1941070000

Axolotl
Lolly Brown
978-0989658430

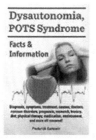

Dysautonomia, POTS
Syndrome
Frederick Earlstein
978-0989658485

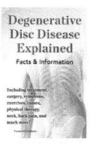

Degenerative Disc
Disease Explained
Frederick Earlstein
978-0989658485

Sinusitis, Hay Fever,
Allergic Rhinitis Explained
Frederick Earlstein
978-1941070024

Wicca
Riley Star
978-1941070130

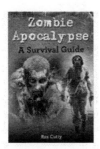

Zombie Apocalypse
Rex Cutty
978-1941070154

Capybara
Lolly Brown
978-1941070062

Eels As Pets
Lolly Brown
978-1941070167

Scabies and Lice Explained
Frederick Earlstein
978-1941070017

Saltwater Fish As Pets
Lolly Brown
978-0989658461

Torticollis Explained
Frederick Earlstein
978-1941070055

Kennel Cough
Lolly Brown
978-0989658409

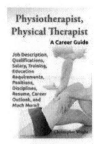

Physiotherapist, Physical
Therapist
Christopher Wright
978-0989658492

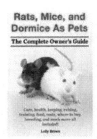

Rats, Mice, and Dormice
As Pets
Lolly Brown
978-1941070079

Wallaby and Wallaroo Care
Lolly Brown
978-1941070031

Bodybuilding Supplements
Explained
Jon Shelton
978-1941070239

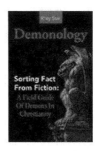

Demonology
Riley Star
978-19401070314

Pigeon Racing
Lolly Brown
978-1941070307

Dwarf Hamster
Lolly Brown
978-1941070390

Cryptozoology
Rex Cutty
978-1941070406

Eye Strain
Frederick Earlstein
978-1941070369

Inez The Miniature Elephant
Asher Ray
978-1941070353

Vampire Apocalypse
Rex Cutty
978-1941070321

29636344R00052

Printed in Great Britain
by Amazon